KT-226-157

Swimming

Rita Storey

W
FRANKLIN WATTS
LONDON•SYDNEY

First published in 2009 by
Franklin Watts
338 Euston Road
London NW1 3BH

Franklin Watts Australia
Level 17/207 Kent Street
Sydney NSW 2000

Words in **bold** are in the glossary on page 30.

Series editor: Sarah Peutrill
Art director: Jonathan Hair

Series designed and created for Franklin Watts by Storeybooks.
Designer: Rita Storey
Editor: Nicola Edwards
Photography: Tudor Photography, Banbury, unless otherwise credited

Picture credits
Bob Martin /Sports Illustrated/Getty p27; i-stock p24; LIU JIN/AFP/Getty Images p21
2008 Getty Images p29

Cover images: Tudor Photography, Banbury.

Thanks to Adam Ruckwood and the Birmingham Swimming Club for the use of their pool. Also thanks to Terri, Dan, Alex and Lauren for their participation in the book.

A CIP catalogue record for this book is available from the British Library.

Dewey classification: 797.2
ISBN: 978 0 7496 8431 0

Printed in China

Franklin Watts is a division of Hachette
Children's Books, an Hachette UK company.
www.hachette.co.uk

Contents

Meet the swimmers   4

Starting out   6

Taking it further   8

The coach   10

In training   12

Training at the pool   14

A good start   16

Technique   18

Injuries and setbacks   20

Lifestyle   22

In competition   24

Sporting heroes   26

The next step   28

Glossary   30

Find out more   31

Index   32

Meet the swimmers

Competitive swimmers race each other over a range of different distances and each swimmer aims to be the fastest. Many people swim in their local swimming pool and on holiday to keep fit or just for fun. However, for a few talented individuals swimming will also become their career. In this book you will meet four swimmers who will share their experiences with you of the training and dedication it takes to perform at the highest level.

Alex Hooper

I am 16 years old and I am a 100m and 200m backstroke swimmer. The thing that drives me most when competing is getting that gold medal. It's a great feeling when you get to stand on the podium and everyone cheers for you, especially when you represent your country. I like competing as part of a team, it is very exciting as you're all in it together and there isn't as much pressure on you as when you compete as an individual.

Coach's comment
Alex represented Great Britain at the European Junior Championships in Belgrade in 2008 where she won a gold medal in the 4x200m freestyle relay. She won a silver medal in the 100m backstroke at the World School Games in Athens in 2006 and she also has many national titles.

Dan Ruckwood

I am 15 years old and I compete in 100m and 200m backstroke events. I like competing as a team more than as an individual, mainly because as a team you know that you have contributed to the success, whereas if you win an individual event, everyone sees you as the 'best'. I don't really like having all the glory just to myself.

Coach's comment
Dan represented England in the Home Countries International in 2007 and has been national 100m and 200m backstroke champion in his age group for the past four years.

Terri Dunning

*I am 23 years old and I am a 100m and 200m butterfly swimmer. Since I began to swim I always wanted to swim faster and achieve **personal best** (PB) times. I enjoy competing in **relay** events as the pressure is on all four swimmers. You still have to perform well though, so that you don't let your team-mates down.*

Coach's comment

Terri has represented Great Britain at World Championships, European Championships and the Commonwealth Games. She won a silver medal in the 4x100m **medley** relay and a bronze medal in the 200m butterfly at the 2006 Commonwealth Games in Melbourne. She also won a gold medal in the 4x100m medley relay at the 2006 European Championships in Budapest. She is the former British record holder in the 100m and 200m butterfly.

Lauren Collins

I am 17 years old and I compete in 100m and 200m freestyle and 200m backstroke events. I am a very competitive person and I love to race, and to win! I enjoy competing as an individual and as a team, but if I had to choose it would be to compete as an individual as that way I put all the work into the race by myself.

Coach's comment

As well as having numerous national titles, Lauren represented Great Britain at the European Junior Championships in 2006 and 2007 where she won three gold medals and two silver medals. She also represented Great Britain at the World Junior Championships in Monterey, California, where she won a silver medal in the 4x200m freestyle relay.

All these swimmers are competing or hoping to compete at the very highest level.

Starting out

Most swimmers enter the competitive side of the sport after learning to swim at their local pool. Many local pools offer swimming lessons and have swimming clubs. If swimmers are keen once they have learnt the basics, they may go on to train and compete for a club in swimming **galas**.

Swimming is also part of the national PE curriculum in England. The aim of the curriculum is for all children to be able to swim a minimum of 25m safely by the time they reach secondary school age.

My mum took me to a mother and toddlers swimming group when I was very young and I was about five years old when I started having swimming lessons. I swam for the school at school galas and joined a club. I swim for Stourbridge Swimming Club, City of Birmingham Swimming Club and for Worcester County.

Terri is swimming the butterfly stroke.

I started swimming when I was quite young. It just involved a couple of sessions a week so I was confident in the water. When I started to compete, it was mainly my mum who encouraged me. My teacher realised I was good so sent me to a local club until I got even better and tried out for City of Birmingham. I also swim for my school team.

I learnt to swim when I was four years old. I started having swimming lessons because my mum wanted me to be able to swim. I got all my badges by the time I was eight. I wanted to carry on swimming, so I joined my local swimming club (Chase Swimming Club) where I started to swim in galas for my club and for Staffordshire County. I moved to the City of Birmingham Swimming Club and swam for the Great Britain senior team in 2004.

For my whole life, I have really enjoyed swimming, but I also enjoy playing cricket and football. I learnt to swim when I was about four years old at my local swimming baths, and then at the age of about six I joined my first swimming club, Redditch SC. I also swim for my school swimming team on a regular basis; we have fixtures against other schools across the country. Because my dad was an Olympic swimmer for Great Britain, he has always urged me into the pool from a young age, and it's just gone on from there; competing at my first county meet, all the way to winning my first national gold medal.

Swimming events

Freestyle
50m
100m
200m
400m
800m (women)
1,500m (men)
Backstroke
100m
200m
Breaststroke
100m
200m
Butterfly
100m
200m
Individual Medley
200m
400m
Freestyle Relay
4x100m
4x200m
Medley Relay
4x100m
Marathon
10km

The strokes

The four strokes that swimmers use in competitive swimming events are butterfly, breaststroke, backstroke and freestyle. Freestyle means any style, but most swimmers choose to swim front crawl as it is the fastest stroke. Swimmers race each other over different distances using one of the four strokes. They may also compete in individual medley races where they swim equal distances of each of the four strokes in one race.

Racing as a team

There are also team relay events in which each member of the team swims a part of the race using one of the four strokes (medley relay) or in freestyle (freestyle relay).

Marathon

Most competitive swimming events take place in a swimming pool but the 10km marathon is an open water swimming event. In open water events competitors swim in lakes, rivers or even in the sea.

Lauren is swimming front crawl.

Taking it further

For swimmers who show particular talent, there are schemes available that give them financial support and allow them to access the best training facilities.

Elite training programmes

The swimmers featured in this book are all members of the City of Birmingham Swimming Club. Terri and Lauren are also part of the British Swimming World Class Programme (WCP). Being on the programme means that Terri and Lauren can continue to study and the UK Sport Athlete Personal Award (APA) they receive will cover the cost of their training.

In addition to the APA, Terri and Lauren are also eligible for support from the English Institute of Sport (EIS) in the West Midlands. The EIS **elite** facilities are based at the Birmingham High Performance Centre at Alexander Stadium. At the centre's state-of-the-art training facilities, swimmers, along with athletes from a range of sports, work with a strength and conditioning coach on their individual development programme. In addition they receive support from **physiotherapists**, **sports psychologists**, **nutritionists** and **performance lifestyle advisors**.

Go for gold

The ultimate prize for a swimmer is a gold medal at the Olympic Games.

Along with track and field athletics, swimming is one of the most popular spectator sports at the Olympic Games and the one with the largest number of events.

When I started competing I had lots of energy to burn off so I could do personal bests very easily, whereas now it is much harder. I decided that swimming was going to be my career when I joined City of Birmingham Swimming Club. To swim there I have to be very committed as I do eight to nine sessions in the pool which is very time consuming so you have to put everything into it.

Alex is swimming backstroke.

When I won my first district gold medal at the age of 10, that's when I thought that I could be a good swimmer if I got my head down and did hard work in the pool. I decided that I wanted to be a swimmer after I won my first national gold medal when I was just 11 years old.

Family support

In all sports, but particularly in swimming, it is important to have the support and encouragement of your family. Swimmers use training pools very early in the morning and with every swimmer who arrives at the pool at 5am for training there is usually a family member who has braved the early start to get them there.

I live with my grandparents and my granddad is the one who takes me training most days.

Coach's notes: support

Family support is very important in swimming, which is quite an expensive and time-consuming sport. If the swimmer's family aren't willing and in a position to commit the time and money, then the child will struggle greatly to succeed.

I started to realise I could be really good at swimming when I started to win all my races at little competitions with Chase. I then started to win races at the County Championships, Midland Districts and National Championships. When I was 14 I was ranked number one for my age group in my event. It was at the Olympic trials in 2004 when I realised I could be really good at my event and I just missed out on making the team for the Olympics. It was then that I decided to really concentrate on the 100m and 200m butterfly. From my performance at the trials, I got put on the World Class Performance Programme. I decided that swimming would be my career when I was put on this programme and given funding to help me train and compete.

Terri is swimming breaststroke. Breaststroke is the slowest of the four swimming strokes.

9

The coach

A good coach is vital to the sustained improvement of a swimmer's performance. The coach is involved with every aspect of the swimmer's training.

The role of the coach

A coach's job is to allow swimmers to reach their maximum potential at just the right time. To do this coaches monitor every aspect of the swimmers' performance and develop a training programme that will increase their fitness and improve their technique. The coach is also there to motivate and support each swimmer.

Adam Ruckwood
Adam has been coaching at the City of Birmingham Swimming Club since 2002. He is a former international swimmer who represented Great Britain at three Olympic Games in 1992, 1996 and 2000. He won a gold medal in the 200m backstroke at the 1994 Commonwealth Games in Canada. He also won silver and bronze medals at the Commonwealth Games, three medals at European Championships and was a finalist at the World Championships five times.

My coach is one of a kind. I get on with him most of the time (obviously you don't agree all the time), but since I've been with him I've really improved.

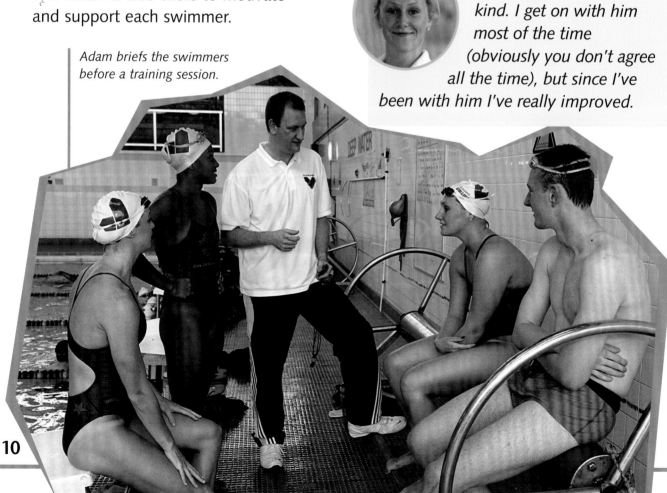

Adam briefs the swimmers before a training session.

Adam and Lauren discuss the outcome of a race.

Performance analysis

Adam insists that the first thing the swimmers do after they have finished a race is sit down and discuss it with him. They look at the **split times** and talk through any aspects of their technique that need improvement. The swimmers can then go and practise any technical aspects that went wrong in the race while it is still fresh in their minds.

Adam also uses video footage to help swimmers to improve their strokes. The swimmers watch videos of past races to see how their technique has developed.

Motivation

Coaches have several different ways of motivating the swimmers they train. Good coaches know their swimmers well and know how to get the best out of each of them. Some swimmers like to be challenged and have set targets, others like competing against others. Some swimmers thrive less on this sort of competitive motivation and prefer to concentrate on achieving personal best times and improving their own performance.

Coach's notes: training

If you are tired or your mind isn't on the training session remember this – your competitors will be training at the same time as you are and if you aren't doing everything correctly and to your best they will beat you next time you compete. Hopefully that will get you training hard!

My coach is also my dad. Having a dad as a coach can be good and bad. Having a family member who has been there before and knows what he's doing is helpful because he can give me tips and ideas of what to do on certain things that I am weak on. It is bad because he can be harder on me in training than he would on other swimmers.

11

In training

Competitive swimmers need to be strong and fit so that they can perform at their best and avoid getting injured. Swimmers use a range of exercises to strengthen their muscles and bring their bodies to a high level of general fitness and flexibility. This means regular training in the gym and on the poolside as well as in the pool.

Core stability training

No matter what stroke they specialise in, swimmers need to do **core stability exercises** to strengthen the muscles in the **trunk** of their bodies. This will also help prevent injuries.

On Tuesdays after the swimming session, the older swimmers (15 years and over) go and do a weights session in the gym. This is just to improve on our strength, mainly for the end of a race when **lactic acid** *kicks in and tires swimmers. We also do just land training every night after the swimming session. This can include using* **medicine balls***, working on improving our strength and power, core stability exercises and flexibility work.*

In this exercise, Lauren is performing a 'plate twist', which develops rotational strength and stability.

Lifting weights helps to build the muscles in Lauren's arms.

I do 30–45 minutes of land training after each evening training session. I also do 60 minutes of land training on a Saturday morning.

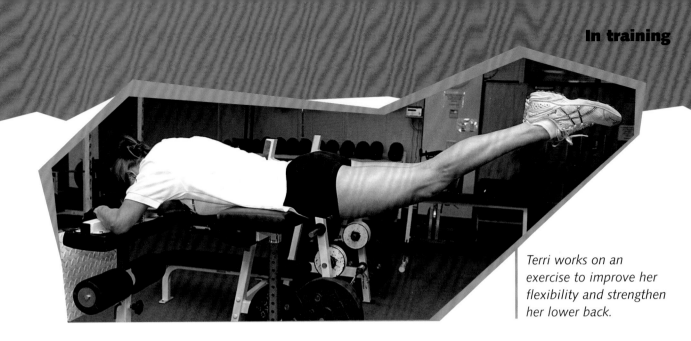

Terri works on an exercise to improve her flexibility and strengthen her lower back.

Weight training

Swimmers need strong arms and shoulders to pull themselves through the water and strong legs to maintain a powerful kick throughout a race. A programme of weight training is worked out for each swimmer which will build up the correct muscles to get maximum power in every stroke.

Flexibility

Swimming puts a lot of strain on the back and spine, especially when swimmers use the **dolphin kick**, either with the butterfly stroke or to power them underwater after they turn. This kick uses a ripple motion through the body and legs and needs a supple spine to make it effective. Swimmers do exercises in the gym and on the poolside to increase the movement and flexibility in their spine.

Adam watches as the swimmers do flexibility exercises at the poolside.

I train for about three hours a week in the gym. I do a lot of flexibility work in the gym and after training which includes a lot of stretching. I also do a lot of core strength for my abdominal muscles and use medicine balls to work my arms.

13

Training at the pool

Swimmers train very hard and very regularly. Morning sessions may start as early as 5am and evening sessions at 4.15pm. Swimmers have to fit their training around their studies and their normal lives.

Warming up on land

Before they get into the pool, the swimmers do a land-based warm-up which is 10 minutes of skipping followed by some arm swings and stretches. Skipping increases the heart rate to prepare the swimmer to perform at a high level. This process is called a **cardiovascular** warm-up.

Warming up in the pool

The swimmers follow their land-based warm-up with a warm-up in the pool, swimming lengths to loosen their bodies. These swimmers warm up over approximately 1,600 metres.

Training session

The main part, or set, of the swimming training will be one of the following:

aerobic – low intensity work including kicking, pulling, technique drills and low level endurance;

threshold – longer-distance swims with short rests aimed at building endurance and stamina. The swimmer's heart works at quite a high rate.

lactate tolerance – very hard, high intensity work, such as maximum effort swims with longer rest periods. The aim is for the swimmers to produce as much lactic acid as possible in their muscles and get used to being able to tolerate the burning sensation it causes without slowing down.

Skipping is an effective warm-up and can be done on the side of the pool before training.

Arm swings help to loosen the arm joints and muscles ready for a swim.

VO2 – maximum intensity swims. VO2 is the maximum volume of oxygen in millilitres you can use in one minute per kilogram of your body weight. If you are fit you have higher VO2 values which means you can exercise more intensely.

Cool-down

The main set is followed by another slower swim to cool down. The cool-down allows the muscles to relax and the heart rate to return to normal. It also reduces the amount of **adrenaline** and lactic acid that build up in the bloodstream when someone exercises very hard.

Training plan

Coaches prepare an annual training plan for the whole season with a breakdown of the competitions in which each swimmer is competing. This plan shows when the swimmers need to be training hard. It is designed to make sure that the swimmers can swim their fastest at the times of year when it really matters, for example at major championships. This annual plan is then broken down into smaller segments – like rungs on a ladder – with the aim of preparing the swimmers to achieve their goals at the end of the year.

I train up to nine sessions a week in the pool, depending on the stage of the season. I do up to four morning sessions from 5 – 7am and five night sessions from 4.15 – 6.15pm. Each session lasts two hours and I have 30 minutes' land work after most night sessions, including core strength exercises and medicine balls. My favourite parts of a training session are the main set, although they are always the hardest parts of the session. It is such a good feeling when you have done a good set and have worked really hard.

Coach's notes: be prepared

It is essential that you arrive early for every training session and you are fully prepared. That means having all the necessary equipment, clothing, drinks, etc. It also means being in the correct frame of mind to listen fully to the coaching staff and train to the best of your ability.

Swimming training means swimming many lengths of the pool every day.

A good start

Getting the best possible start to a race is vital for winning. Different strokes need different starting techniques.

A backstroke start

A backstroke race starts in the water. Swimmers hold the bar on the **starting block** and place their feet on the wall about 20cm apart. They push on their feet just before the start so that their legs are at a 90 degree angle at the knees. As the starting gun goes off the swimmers push with their hands away from the blocks and drive with their legs. Their backs arch as they dive backwards through the air, hitting the water first with their hands, then with their heads and lastly with the rest of their bodies.

Dive starts

Freestyle, butterfly and breaststroke races start with a dive from the blocks. The key to a good starting dive is to get off the blocks as quickly as possible, travel through the air as far as possible and enter the water as cleanly as possible. As swimmers enter the water, they aim to keep streamlined with their hands one on top of another and their arms held tightly over their ears.

Dan and Alex perform the two stages of a backstroke start.

A backstroke start is almost like a backwards dive. You arch your back and enter the water with your hands first followed by your body. The idea is to get up-and-over the water. It is faster to go over the water than through it because of the water resistance.

Learning to glide as fast as possible underwater can gain crucial time in a race.

After the dive start comes a glide through the water, followed by a further underwater phase using a dolphin kick. Swimmers can travel faster underwater using the dolphin kick than they can swim on the top of the water. Swimming race rules allow a swimmer to travel up to 15m underwater from every start and turn before surfacing, so swimmers work constantly on this technique in training to gain extra speed.

Relay races

In a relay race the timing of their dives is crucial for the second, third and fourth swimmers. They are allowed to be completely stretched out over the water as long as their toes are still on the block when the incoming swimmer touches the wall. This makes it vital that they judge exactly when the incoming swimmer is beginning the last arm stroke and when he or she will make contact with the wall.

Timing the dive at the change-over in a relay race takes a lot of practice.

Technique

Swimmers have a lot of things to think about when they are perfecting their swimming technique: their legs, arms, breathing and timing are the main ones. An efficient swimming stroke means less wasted energy and a faster time.

Legs and arms

The leg kicks used in each stroke are not only a way of pushing swimmers through the water but also a way of controlling their body position as they swim. The legs play a bigger part in some strokes than others. In backstroke the leg kick is an important part of propelling swimmers through the water, while in freestyle the arms provide the main force. Swimmers aim to perfect the timing between their arm and leg movements to create maximum speed.

Breathing

It is vital to breathe as you are swimming. Taking the right number of breaths without slowing down is a technique that all swimmers try to perfect. Freestyle and butterfly swimmers are trained not to take a breath when coming up to the finish of a race. When swimmers turn their heads to breathe it slows them down very slightly, so when they are in a race not taking that last breath can make all the difference.

Butterfly swimmers practise taking a breath without losing speed.

Timing

Practising the timing of all swimming strokes is important, but the timing of the butterfly stroke is one of the most difficult to master. Most swimmers make two leg kicks to one arm stroke and breathe either on every stroke or on alternate strokes.

Turns

Precious fractions of a second can be gained by making a good turn in a race. Swimmers learn different types of turn depending on the stroke they are swimming.

Pivot turn The pivot turn is used in both butterfly and breaststroke races. The race rules say that swimmers must touch the wall with both hands as they turn so swimmers touch with their arms outstretched then spin round and push off hard with their feet.

Freestyle and front crawl turn To make this turn, swimmers approach the wall and do a forward somersault just before they reach it. They place their feet on wall and stretch their arms out, then they push hard on the wall and twist onto their fronts. Timing the somersault to give a powerful push-off against the wall is crucial.

Backstroke turn The hardest thing for swimmers making the backcrawl turn is knowing when they are nearing the wall. Some swimmers count how many strokes it takes to get from one end of the pool to the other, leaving themselves with the space to make a tumble turn.

Alex practises a tumble turn. This turn is used in freestyle and backstroke races.

Coach's notes: the finish
Swimmers must get their heads down, not take a breath, focus on the wall and try to make sure they finish on a full stroke. Terri won her Commonwealth bronze medal by only 8/100ths of a second - about the length of a finger nail! That shows how important the finish is.

19

Injuries and setbacks

All swimmers suffer setbacks at some time in their career. A loss of form or getting injured are always tough, especially if a swimmer has been training hard and well and is expecting a good result or performance. The determination to deal with setbacks can make the difference between a good swimmer and a great one.

Loss of form

If swimmers understand why their performance was not as good as they wanted it to be, they can work on putting it right. Their coach and a sports psychologist can offer practical help and encouragement, while the support of other swimmers, friends and family is also important.

Injuries

Swimming can be a very safe form of exercise as the water supports the body, unlike running

When a team-mate has performed badly you still act the same around them, but it doesn't hurt to give them a hug and tell them to keep their chin up! I think everyone goes through a rough patch in their career. You go through a point of giving up but you have to keep looking on the bright side. If I did give up I would probably get really fat!

Arun, the strength and conditioning coach, discusses the day's training with Terri before she starts her work-out.

I had a bad injury to my back at the end of 2003. I had to have a couple of months out of the water in order to recover. I had to strengthen the lower part of my back by doing core strength exercises and regular stretching. It was frustrating to not be in the water, knowing I was missing training and competitions.

where an athlete's feet are constantly making contact with a hard surface. However, that does not mean that swimming is injury-free for competitive swimmers who are training hard. The repetitive moves made by the shoulders, elbows and knees and the constant flexing of the back mean that these areas are very prone to injury. Strength and conditioning coaches help swimmers to work on strengthening these parts of the body to help avoid injury to them. Specialist sports physiotherapists are on hand to help if an injury does occur.

Just the beginning

Some people overcome major setbacks in their lives to become competitive swimmers. The Paralympic Games take place in the same year as the Olympic Games and are an elite sporting event for swimmers with disabilities.

I have had a few setbacks during my swimming career. I broke my knee when I was 13 years old playing in a rugby match for my school team, and then I broke the same knee playing basketball the following year. The first time I broke my knee, I was out of the swimming pool for around four months. I had about two to three months of physiotherapy to get my knee back fully fit again.

Thirteen-year-old Eleanor Simmonds won two gold medals at the Paralympic Games in Beijing in 2008. She was born with achondroplasia, or dwarfism.

21

Lifestyle

Swimmers have a very different lifestyle to other young people of their age. They have very little time to themselves because of the amount of time they have to spend training and getting to and from the pool. This means that seeing friends and socialising can be difficult to fit in. Most evenings are taken up with training and weekends are spent catching up with homework or being away at swimming competitions. This can be hard on the swimmers, but they are pursuing a dream and none of them would change their lifestyle.

Eating to be fit

A healthy, balanced diet is essential to succeed in swimming. At least five portions of fruit and vegetables a day are essential for providing the nutrients and minerals needed. Along with these, a high carbohydrate and low fat intake is necessary to give the body the energy to train well each day. No food is banned, and swimmers can eat chocolate or other 'goodies' as long as they limit them to occasional 'treats'.

Once I knew that I wanted to be a professional swimmer, I knew that I had to stop playing football and rugby because of the risk of an injury. Yes, it is a sacrifice to make, but when you want to excel at a certain sport you understand why you need to make sacrifices.

My mum takes care of my diet and makes sure that I eat enough protein and carbohydrates. I do allow myself treats but that has to stop! Our coach weighs us each week to make sure that we are staying the same weight.

Swimmers need to eat plenty of carbohydrates and vegetables. This colourful salad combines both.

As a teenager I thought I missed out on things such as going out with my friends to parties as I was always swimming, but as I have got older, I realise that I have got plenty of time to do normal things in the future and I would not change a thing.

It is important that the swimmers have a small snack immediately after they finish training, as the muscles are more susceptible to taking on carbohydrate straight after a training session. This quick intake of carbohydrates will help them recover ready for the next training session.

Water, water everywhere!

Drinking throughout training is also vitally important. Swimmers lose a lot of sweat during training but, as they are in the water and already wet, they don't notice the amount of fluid they lose. Being dehydrated can have a negative impact on performance, so the swimmers have plenty of drinks with them on the poolside.

I do miss out on going out with friends, but I get to travel the world and meet new people. When I'm standing on the podium and the British flag is going up and my mum is crying because she is so proud, that's the moment that makes it all worthwhile.

There are no set rules about when swimmers should eat before a competition or training session. However, if they eat too close to the session it can make them feel sick, so coaches advise them to leave an hour and a half between eating a big meal and swimming.

Education

Swimmers can combine their training with schoolwork. Most of the swimmers that Adam coaches are studying for exams at school and one is at university. The two-hour morning training sessions start at 5am and the evening sessions at 4.15pm so fitting everything in takes hard work and dedication.

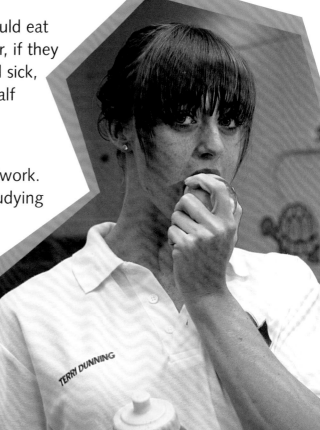

Swimmers keep plenty of water and healthy snacks with them when they are training.

In competition

The preparation for a competition is both mental and physical. The training for a big race is designed so that swimmers are at the peak of their physical and mental fitness at just the right moment.

The season

The swimming season usually starts in late August or early September. Swimmers do not compete during the early part of the season as they are getting back into training, getting fit and working on the technical aspects of their swimming.

Short and long course

In the early part of the season the majority of competitions are 'short course', which means the races take place in a 25m pool. In the early part of the following year there are more 'long course' competitions, which are swum in 50m pools. The Olympic Games and Commonwealth Games are held in 50m pools.

The major games or national championships are held in late July and early August. After that the swimmers take a break for three weeks to recharge their batteries.

Coach's notes: relaxation

I encourage my swimmers to not go near a swimming pool in their summer break! I feel it is important they come back refreshed and ready for the new season so it is good to forget about swimming and relax. I try and stress to them to not go mad and eat everything in sight or they will have to work a lot harder in the early season to get back in shape. Not all of them listen to me though!

At the start of a race the swimmers must try to block out all the noises and distractions and focus their minds on winning.

Mental preparation

Before important events such as Olympic trials or national championships, Adam brings in a psychologist to help the swimmers he coaches with their mental preparation. The psychologist helps the swimmers to feel less nervous and more positive about their races by creating aims and goals for them to achieve.

Tapering

Before major races, coaches gradually reduce the amount of training and concentrate on stroke technique and race strategy. This allows the swimmers' muscles to recover and give their maximum performance in the competition.

Personal bests

As well as trying to win races, swimmers constantly aim to improve their race times. A swimmer may lose a very fast race but still be delighted with the outcome if he or she achieves a personal best.

Having a race plan

Winning a race is not just about swimming as fast as possible for the whole race. Short sprint races may be all about swimmers powering off the blocks, but a longer race is won or lost by how well swimmers judge not only their speed but also their ability to race at that speed right to the finish line. Burning up all their energy at the start may mean that they are overtaken at the end.

Coach's notes: success

Talent is an extremely important factor in whether a swimmer succeeds or not, but there are masses of other aspects which are important. Determination, dedication, drive and will to win can also affect whether or not the swimmer succeeds.

Depending on the competition, a personal best is sometimes as good as winning. If you have achieved a personal best you know that you have done the best you have ever done and you can't be disappointed with that.

If you are too aggressive at the start of the race you could tire towards the end and lose valuable time, but if you pace it through the race and keep up with the leading pack, you'll have some extra energy left in the tank to accelerate in the last 25m or 50m.

Sporting heroes

Successful swimmers are an inspiration to those who are training hard to reach the top of their sport. Swimming heroes may be world champions, Olympic gold medallists or equally they may be swimmers in a local club who have shown dedication and commitment to their sport.

Fair competition

Swimmers train very hard to be the best they possibly can. Unfortunately in swimming, as in other sports, there are a few competitors who cheat by using drugs to improve their performance. All drugs that could give an athlete an unfair advantage are banned.

My first swimming heroes were probably some of the older swimmers from my club when I was about 10. I looked up to them and I thought to myself that I would never be as fast as them. Now I am faster than all of them!

My first swimming hero was Ian Thorpe. I watched him swim at the Olympic Games and he was amazing, winning all his events and breaking records.

My first swimming hero was probably my dad. I grew up with him being away on GB camps abroad, seeing him compete all over the world and winning at senior nationals and thinking that he was the 'best' in the world; I was about five years old at the time! I think every swimmer in the world looks up to Michael Phelps now, after the 2008 Beijing Olympics. Every swimmer's dream is to win an Olympic gold medal, let alone eight!

Ian Thorpe
(Australia)
Events: 100m, 200m, 400m, 800m freestyle; 100m backstroke, 200m individual medley.

*Olympic gold medals:
Sydney 2000, 100m freestyle, 400m freestyle, 4x100m freestyle relay.
Athens 2004 400m freestyle, 200m freestyle.*

Nicknamed 'The Thorpedo', and one of the greatest swimmers ever, Ian Thorpe has won five Olympic gold medals and 11 world titles.

Swimmers are regularly tested to see if there are any of these illegal drugs in their bodies. A swimmer who is found to have taken drugs risks being banned from the sport.

I admire Michael Phelps for obvious reasons, but not just because he got eight golds at the Beijing Olympics; it is because a lot of people doubted that he would get that many. Michael Phelps has a great underwater kick which gives him an advantage over other swimmers. I also have that kick but I don't use it to its full potential which means I could go a lot faster. He also has a fantastic long and powerful stroke which means he can grab more water and pull forward more.

Michael Phelps
(USA)
Events: freestyle, butterfly, individual medley, medley relay and freestyle relay.

Olympic gold medals:
Athens 2004, six gold medals:
400m individual medley, 200m butterfly, 200m individual medley, 100m butterfly, 4x200m freestyle relay and 4x100m medley relay.
Beijing 2008, eight gold medals:
400m individual medley, 4x100m freestyle relay, 200m freestyle, 200m butterfly, 4x200m freestyle relay, 200m individual relay,100m butterfly and 4x100m medley relay.

Michael Phelps has won 14 Olympic gold medals, the most of any Olympian. He also holds seven world swimming records.

Michael Phelps swims breaststroke in a 200m individual medley race in Beijing.

The next step

Training to be a top-level competitive swimmer is a long, steady process. The early mornings and constant training regime will be too much for some. Some will get injured or lose momentum and for others life may move in other directions. Many will remain involved in swimming in some other way, perhaps through training or coaching.

My ambition is to make the Olympics and get a gold medal. If I do that all the hard work would have paid off. I also would like to hold a world record sometime in my career. My next target is to make the Commonwealth team. I will get to my target by stepping up my training sessions and not cutting any corners. In five years I see myself ending my swimming career with a gold medal at the Olympics, as after this there is nothing else which needs to be done. All athletes dream of winning at the Olympics and this would be my dream fulfilled. In swimming there is only a lot of money to be made if you are the best of the best, but money isn't the issue with me. I would rather have that single gold medal than millions of pounds.

Eyes on the prize

Every swimmer's dream is to win a gold medal at the Olympic Games and all the swimmers in this book are striving to achieve that ambition.

My ultimate ambition, almost every swimmer's dream, is to win Olympic gold, but if I was being reasonable, my dream would to make the GB Olympic Team; just making the team would be absolutely amazing! My next target is to make the GB Schools Team. To get on the team, I need to qualify for the International Schools Team which means coming first or second in the English Schools Team – a long process, but representing Great Britain makes it all worthwhile.

In five years' time I see myself having achieved the best I can in my swimming career and having no regrets.

My ultimate ambition is to win an Olympic gold medal. My next target is to improve each year and qualify at the Olympic trials. I will train hard and try not to let anything get in my way.

British swimmer Rebecca Adlington shows her two Olympic gold medals after the Beijing Olympic Games.

The last Olympics have inspired me to carry on swimming, as a British girl won two golds so I know that it can be done.

The last Olympics have made me realise how proud I am to be a swimmer and it shows that all the cold and early mornings can be worth it in the end!

Slowly but surely

Dan, Alex and Lauren are looking forward to a long and successful career in swimming. Breaking world records and winning medals are all part of their dream. Terri has already achieved a great deal in her career and is still hoping to achieve her ultimate goal of a medal at the Olympic Games. Let's wish them all the best of luck.

Glossary

adrenaline A hormone that is released into the bloodstream in response to physical or mental stress. It stimulates the body to perform at its maximum level.

cardiovascular Involving the heart and blood vessels.

core stability exercises Exercises that strengthen the core muscles in the trunk of the body to help prevent injuries.

dolphin kick A kick used in the butterfly stroke where the legs are held together and moved up and down with the knees slightly bent on the upward swing.

elite The very best of a group of people.

gala A type of swimming contest.

lactic acid A substance produced in the muscles during exercise. Too much lactic acid can cause cramping pains.

medicine ball A large, heavy ball, thrown from one person to another for exercise.

medley A mixture. In a medley relay race each length is swum using a different stroke: butterfly, backstroke, breaststroke and freestyle.

nutritionist A trained specialist who advises athletes on what they should eat and drink.

performance lifestyle advisor A person who advises athletes about lifestyle choices.

personal best Sometimes shortened to PB, a swimmer's best ever time in a race.

physiotherapist A trained specialist who deals with injuries using massage, exercises and other physical treatments.

relay A race between teams in which each member only swims part of the distance.

split times The time it takes to complete set distances in a longer race, for example 50m and 100m in a 200m race.

sports psychologist An expert in how the mind of an athlete works. Sports psychologists help athletes believe they can win.

starting block A raised platform at one end of a pool from which swimmers begin a race.

trunk The main body of a person excluding the head, arms and legs.

Find out more

Websites

www.brianmac.co.uk/swimming
Information on a range of swimming training and swimming techniques.

http://news.bbc.co.uk/sport1/hi/olympics/swimming/default.stm
News about swimming events and swimmers' achievements from the BBC.

www.fina.org
The website of the international governing body of swimming, with information about current swimmers, records, world rankings and much more.

www.britishswimming.org
The home site of British swimming, diving, water polo and synchronised swimming. It has links to clubs and leisure centres to help you find all the information you need to know about learning to swim, joining a club or just swimming for pleasure.

www.swimmingworldmagazine.com
Up-to-date news stories from the world of swimming, plus interviews with current stars and all the latest results.

Books

Know Your Sport: Swimming, Paul Mason (Franklin Watts, 2008)
A guide to swimming, with step-by-step photographs and explanations of some of the strokes as well as profiles and statistics giving information about some of the world's greatest swimmers.

Sporting Skills: Swimming, Clive Gifford (Wayland, 2008)
A step-by-step guide to your favourite sport. It introduces techniques and includes advice on training, equipment and resources.

Index

Adlington, Rebecca   29
adrenaline   15, 30
aerobic training   14
ambition   28–9
arms   12, 13, 14, 16, 17,
        18, 19

backstroke   7, 8, 16, 18, 19
breaststroke   7, 9, 16, 19,
        27
breathing   18–19
butterfly   6, 7, 13, 16,
        18–19

cardiovascular warm-ups
        14, 30
coaches   8, 10–11, 20, 21
Commonwealth Games   24,
        28
competition   24–5
cool-down   15
core stability exercises   12,
        30

diet   22–3
dive starts   16–17
dolphin kick   13, 17, 30
drugs   26–7

education   6, 23
elite training programmes   8
endurance   14
events   7

family support   9
finish   19
flexibility   13

freestyle   7, 16, 18–19
front crawl   7, 19

galas   6, 30
gliding underwater   17

heroes   26–7

injuries   20–1

lactate tolerance   14
lactic acid   12, 14, 15, 30
land training   12–13
legs   13, 16, 18, 19
lifestyle   22–3, 30
long course   24

marathons   7
medicine balls   12, 13, 30
medley races   7, 30
mental preparation   25
motivation   11

Olympic Games   8, 24, 28,
        29
open water events   7

Paralympic Games   21
performance analysis   11,
        30
personal bests   8, 25, 30
Phelps, Michael   27
physiotherapy   21
pivot turns   19
pool training   14–15

race plans   25

relaxation   24
relay races   5, 7, 17, 30
Ruckwood, Adam   10–11

season   24
setbacks   20–1
short course   24
Simmonds, Eleanor   21
skipping   14
split times   11, 30
sports psychologists   20,
        25, 30
stamina   14
starting blocks   16, 30
starts   16–17, 24
strength and conditioning
        8, 20, 21
strokes   7, 11, 13, 18, 19,
        27
success   25
swimming lessons   6

tapering   25
team events   4, 5, 7
technique   18–19, 25
Thorpe, Ian   26
threshold training   14
timing   19
training   11, 12–13, 14–15
tumble turns   19
turns   16, 19

VO2   15

warming up   14
weight training   12, 13